mac*tracks*

Tomorrow [illegible] tter

Akberali Manji

MACMILLAN

mac*tracks*

First published 1998 by
MACMILLAN EDUCATION LTD
London and Basingstoke
Companies and representatives throughout the world

ISBN 0–333–66004–8

This book is printed on paper suitable for recycling and made from fully managed and sustained forest sources.

10 9 8 7 6 5 4 3 2 1
07 06 05 04 03 02 01 00 99 98

Printed in China

A catalogue record for this book is available from the British Library.

Series editor: Lorna Evans

Illustrations by Donald Harley/B. L. Kearley Ltd

Chapter 1

Joseph Kuleba was twelve years old. He lived with his family in a two-room flat in Kurasini, near the warm blue waters of the Indian Ocean.

It was nearly six o'clock, and Joseph was standing on the small balcony outside the flat. He looked down at the street. His big brother, Ben, would be coming home soon.

Ben had left school, and today, like most days, he was out on his bicycle, looking for a job. In the evenings he taught Joseph how to ride the bicycle.

They went up and down the narrow street. Ben held on to the bicycle, while Joseph turned the pedals. Up and down they went, laughing and wobbling, until Joseph learned to ride the bicycle all on his own.

Joseph loved riding that bicycle.

"Maybe one day I'll have a bicycle, too," he said to himself. "Then I won't be late for school."

Joseph was a pupil at Mkunguni primary school. He was not top of his class, but he was not bottom either. He liked school. But he was often late and so he got into trouble. Today Joseph's teacher had sent a letter to his father about it.

Mr Kuleba was reading the letter now. He called Joseph indoors.

"You're late because you take too long to get to school, Joseph," Mr Kuleba said. "What are you going to do about it?"

"If I had a bicycle . . ." Joseph began.

"Now, Joseph. You know that's not possible," said his father. "We don't have money for bicycles in this family. We need money for important things – food, medicine and school uniforms for you and your little sister."

"Ben has a bicycle," said Joseph.

"Ben bought that bicycle with his own money," said his father.

That was true. For two years Ben had helped their neighbour, Mr Hassan, in his small shop after school and on Saturdays and Sundays. He had saved the money for his bicycle.

Joseph's father would not talk about it any more.

"You must learn to walk more quickly, that's all," he said. "And be early tomorrow – I don't want any more letters."

Joseph went back to the little balcony. He liked to come here when he was unhappy. He could sit by himself and think.

He had some pots on the balcony, where he grew tomato plants. He liked to grow plants, and he loved tomatoes.

Joseph sat down by his tomato plants. He watched the people in the street below. Everybody was busy, and everybody was happy, except for him.

If only he had a bicycle, everything would be better.

Joseph had not been on the balcony for very long when he saw Ben. Ben was riding his bicycle up the street. He stopped, got off his bicycle, and carried it in from the street.

Joseph heard voices indoors, and a few minutes later Ben came out onto the balcony.

"What happened?" he asked. "Are you in trouble again?"

Joseph told him about the letter. Then he added, "I need a bicycle. Please let me ride your bicycle to school."

"Don't be silly," Ben answered. "I ride that bicycle every day. I need it myself, to look for work. You'll have to wait until you're older."

"It will be too late by then!" said Joseph. "I need a bicycle now, to go to school."

"No, you don't." Ben smiled. "Tell me what you did this morning."

"Well, I did sleep too long," Joseph said. "Then I couldn't find my bag, and all my books were in it. Then I couldn't find my pencil box. I needed that, too. It took a long time to get ready."

Ben laughed.

"It's all very well for you," Joseph said. "You don't have to walk to school."

"I walked to the same school when I was twelve," Ben told him. "Which way do you go?"

"I always go down the street to the beach first of all. Then I walk along the beach, and through the town to school."

"And do you stop in the port? Do you watch the ships?"

"Well, yes," said Joseph. He loved the sea and the ships from far away places.

"And do you stop to look at the shops?"

"Well, yes." Joseph thought about the bicycle shop. He had stood outside it for a long time that morning.

"You know what you have to do, don't you?" Ben said.

"Yes," said Joseph slowly. "I have to get up early, find my things quickly, and walk straight to school. And I mustn't watch the ships or stop in the town."

"That's right," Ben told him.

He stood up. "Now water your tomato plants, and then come inside. Food's ready."

Chapter 2

The next morning Joseph was up early.

He picked up his clean clothes and hurried out of the room to the water tap. He washed quickly and put on his clean clothes for school. His father had already gone to work.

"Here's your breakfast," his mother told him. "Drink your tea while it's still hot."

Then she went to help Joseph's little sister get ready for school.

As soon as Joseph had eaten he lifted up his big green school bag. His books and a pencil box full of pens and pencils were already in it.

"I won't be late today," he said to himself. "There's lots of time. Nothing will go wrong. I won't get into trouble."

Then he thought for a minute and added, "But I still wish I had a bicycle."

Joseph walked down the little street to the beach. The sun was already hot on his back, so he stopped for a while. He looked at the sea. He listened to the wind in the trees. He even sat down.

"I'll rest, just for a minute," he said to himself.

Near to him on the beach the waves were tiny, but further out to sea the waves were larger and the sea was rough.

Those waves were dangerous. Joseph knew there were sharks out there – big, hungry fish which would attack almost anything. Uncle Juma had told him all about sharks.

Joseph got up and walked on, past the line of small boats that belonged to the fishermen. A few rich people kept their big boats there as well.

Joseph saw his uncle's boat at the end of the line. Uncle Juma was a fisherman. He was sitting on the sandy beach near the boat, mending his fishing nets.

Joseph greeted him politely.

"Are you on your way to school, Joseph?" asked Uncle Juma. "Don't be late."

"There's lots of time," said Joseph. "I'll just sit down for a minute."

He sat down beside his uncle.

"Will you take me out in your boat this afternoon, Uncle Juma? I can come here after school."

"Yes," said his uncle. "If you come this afternoon, I'll take you out. We can catch a fish for your dinner. Now off you go. Hurry up, or you'll be late for school."

"I really need a bicycle," Joseph told him, but Uncle Juma just laughed.

Joseph walked on again, past the gate to the harbour. Big ships from far away could be safe in the harbour. The sea there was deep and dark, but it was never rough.

The harbour was always busy. Joseph waited while a lorry passed through the gate.

A new ship had tied up in the harbour the night before. He stopped. Where had the new ship come from? What was it carrying?

"I've got lots of time," Joseph thought. "I'll just watch for a minute."

A few minutes later Joseph walked on through the town. In the market there were big green coconuts, and yellow mangos, and peppers, red and green. There were tomatoes like the ones he grew on the balcony at home.

He walked past the shops. There was new bread in the first shop, and books and maps in the second shop,

and cups and saucers and plates in a third. He could hear loud music in the next shop. He tried to pass the shops quickly, but it was no good. More time was lost.

And then there was the bicycle shop!

By the time Joseph was near the school, he was no longer early. The bell had not yet rung, but the other children were already in the school yard. Joseph was all alone in the road, except for a dirty, brown dog.

The dog was the first thing that went wrong for Joseph that day. Nobody loved that dog. Young boys were always chasing it and throwing stones at it. It hated all boys.

As Joseph came nearer, the dog got very angry. It stood up, opened its mouth, and growled. It had big yellow teeth, teeth that would bite hard.

Joseph saw the dog just in time. He ran to the nearest tree and climbed up it as fast as he could. As he ran, he dropped his bag in the middle of the dusty road. His books and his pencil box fell out.

The dog ran up to the tree. It growled and barked and jumped up at the tree after Joseph. When it could not catch him it sat under the tree and barked.

"Go away," Joseph cried, but the dog just barked and growled at him.

Joseph sat in the tree for a long time. He would be late for school. His teacher would be angry. There would be another letter to his father.

But what could he do? The dog was still at the foot of the tree. If he jumped down the dog would catch him. Those big yellow teeth would bite him.

There was nothing for it. He would just have to wait.

Chapter 3

After a while, Joseph heard something. A bell was ringing.

He pushed the leaves of the tree to one side so that he could see better. A boy on a bicycle was riding along the road to the school.

It was Philip.

Philip was in the same class as Joseph, but the two boys were not friends. Joseph did not like Philip, and Philip did not like Joseph.

Philip's father was rich. He had a big house and a fast car. Because of this Philip thought that he was better than the other children. He was always making trouble for poor boys like Joseph.

"Philip!" called Joseph. "Help me! Save me from this dog! It's going to attack me. It's going to bite me if I come down."

There was no answer. Philip did not even look up at Joseph.

"Help!" Joseph shouted again. "Please help me, Philip."

Philip stopped and got off his bicycle. He was afraid of the dog, too. It was still waiting under Joseph's tree, barking loudly.

Philip bent down and picked up Joseph's pencil box from the middle of the road.

"It's a good thing I found this!" he laughed. "I left my pencil box at home. Don't be late for school, Joseph! You don't want to get into trouble, do you?"

Joseph could only watch as Philip rode off to school.

Now he was late and he had no pencil box either. He felt very unhappy.

But one good thing happened. The dog chased Philip's bicycle. It ran off down the road after Philip. When it could not catch him it gave up and walked away.

Joseph climbed down the tree and picked up his bag and his books. His shirt was dirty now and he had a cut on his knee. He felt very sorry for himself.

He walked slowly along the road. He did not want to go into his classroom. He knew what would happen there. His teacher would be angry and the other children would laugh at him.

Something moved in front of Joseph, by his feet. He looked down and saw a little lizard, brown with yellow spots. It was almost the same colour as the dusty road.

The lizard ran away from Joseph, then sat still. It looked at him.

Joseph thought the lizard was beautiful. He stopped and looked at it. And then he saw something in the grass at the side of the road.

He bent down to see better. It was a wallet.

Joseph forgot all about the lizard, which ran away as fast as it could. He picked up the wallet and opened it. It was full of money. Joseph had never seen so much money in his whole life.

He put the wallet into his bag.

"I'll give it to the headmaster," he thought to himself. "Someone has dropped it near the school. Perhaps the headmaster knows who it belongs to. I'll give the wallet to him at break time."

When at last Joseph walked into his classroom the other boys had started their first lesson. All of them were busy.

Their teacher had drawn a map on the blackboard. The children were copying the map into their books. Some of them had finished already.

Joseph tried to slip into the room quietly. He did not want anyone to see him. He knew that he would be in trouble again.

It was no good.

"Look!" shouted Philip. "Here's Joseph! He's even later than I was!"

All the pupils in the class turned round.

"Late again!" one of Philip's friends called out, and all the other pupils laughed.

Joseph's teacher was very angry with him.

"All the other children got here early," she told him. "And look at your clothes. Joseph, you're a very naughty boy."

Joseph tried to tell her what had happened.

"I'm very sorry. I *was* early," he began," but a dog chased me up a tree, and . . ."

"The dog chased Philip," said the teacher. "Philip has already told me all about it."

"No! The dog chased me, not Philip!" Joseph cried.

"That's not true!" answered Philip. "Joseph's just lazy. That is why he's late."

The teacher would not listen to Joseph.

"Be quiet," she told him. "I don't want to hear another word from you. Just sit down and get on with your work. Copy this map of Africa from the blackboard."

Chapter 4

That was the next bad thing that happened to Joseph. How could he copy a map when Philip had stolen his pencils?

"Please," he began, "I can't draw a map. Philip stole my pencil box and all my pencils."

"No I didn't!" cried Philip. "This is my pencil box! My father bought it for me."

Joseph walked over to Philip and took a pencil out of the box.

"Look!" shouted Philip. "He's stolen one of my pencils!"

"I haven't stolen anything. They're my pencils!" Joseph answered. "And that's my pencil box."

"Sit down," said the teacher angrily. "If you boys can't be good, I shall send you to see the headmaster. There'll be *real* trouble then."

Both boys were quiet. They were afraid of the headmaster. All the children in the school were afraid of him.

"Get on with your work," the teacher went on. "I don't want to hear another word from either of you. You're not to talk about dogs, or pencil boxes, or anything."

Joseph sat down and tried to draw the map. He was so angry he could not do his work well. His hands were dirty and made his book dirty, too.

He could not make the rivers blue and the mountains brown either. Philip still had all his coloured pencils. It wasn't fair.

INDIAN
OCEAN
SOUTH EAST AFR

His teacher walked round the classroom, looking at the maps which the pupils had drawn. She stopped by Joseph's desk and looked at his book.

"That map is not good enough," she told him. "You must stay behind after school today for half an hour. You can draw a better map than that, Joseph. I know you can do it. You usually draw good maps."

All morning things went wrong for Joseph. He was in trouble all the time.

He got most of his sums wrong.

He could not find the right page in his reading book.

He broke the pencil that he had taken from Philip.

He had forgotten to bring his library book to school.

He dropped his rubber on the floor. It rolled away and he could not find it again.

He thought that the morning would never end, but then, at last, the school bell rang. It was time for the morning break.

Joseph hurried out of the classroom. He did not want to talk to anybody, even the boys who were his friends. He just wanted to be alone for a while.

When Joseph was in trouble at school, he always went outside. He always sat under a big, green mango tree, which was heavy with leaves. For him it was like the balcony at home. He could be alone there, and think.

The mango tree was very near to the window of the headmaster's room.

The other children usually stayed away from the mango tree. They thought that a big green snake lived there.

Joseph sat down by the tree and closed his eyes. He wanted to forget everything that had happened that morning. He even forgot about the wallet.

"Joseph!"

Somebody was calling him.

Joseph looked up. Philip was standing nearby with his friends. They were all laughing.

"Come here, Joseph!" said Philip.

Joseph got to his feet.

"What do you want?" he asked.

"I want to give you your pencil box," said Philip.

All his friends laughed again, louder this time. They were going to do something nasty, Joseph just knew it.

He waited under the tree.

"Bring the pencil box to me here," he said at last.

"All right!" said Philip. "Here it is! Catch it!"

He threw the box at Joseph.

Joseph tried to catch his pencil box, but it was too high and too fast. It flew right past him, above his head.

The pencil box went through the window of the headmaster's room. The window was open.

CRASH!

Philip and his friends ran away as fast as they could.

Joseph's feet would not run. He just stood by the window, waiting for more trouble.

Chapter 5

Joseph did not have to wait long. The headmaster came out of his office. He was holding the pencil box tightly in his hand.

"Joseph Kuleba!" called the headmaster.

"Yes, sir?"

"Is this your pencil box?" asked the headmaster angrily.

"Yes, sir," answered Joseph sadly.

"What happened? Why did you throw it through my window?"

"I didn't throw it, sir. It wasn't me."

"Then who did throw it?" asked the headmaster. "There are no other boys here."

He was right. Philip and his friends had run away. Joseph was all alone, under the mango tree.

"Well, this is your pencil box, Joseph Kuleba," the headmaster went on. "And it came through my window. You're the only boy here. Did you throw it?"

Joseph had no time to answer.

"A pencil box is not a football, Joseph," the headmaster was saying. "Only a very foolish boy would throw a pencil box around. There might have been a very bad accident."

The headmaster looked down at Joseph. He seemed very big. Joseph was afraid.

"You might have broken the window," the headmaster went on. "You might have hit me on the head. What would you do then? Did you think about that?"

"I don't know, sir," said Joseph. "It wasn't..."

"Don't say another word," the headmaster broke in. "I don't want to hear. You're going to stay here this afternoon, after school has finished. You have some very big lessons to learn, Joseph Kuleba."

"My teacher has already told me to stay in after school for half an hour after school, sir," said Joseph, very quietly.

He was feeling very unhappy.

"Then you'll have to stay for one whole hour," the headmaster told him. "That's half an hour for your teacher and half an hour for me," he added.

After the morning break, it was time for a sports lesson.

"This time things will go right for me," thought Joseph. "I shan't get into any more trouble."

Joseph was one of the best runners in school. He ran every night after school, and sometimes on Saturdays and Sundays too.

He often ran along the soft golden sands of the beach. His legs were strong, and he did not often get tired. He knew he could run faster than all the other boys in his class. He nearly always came first in races.

But that day things went wrong for Joseph even in his sports lesson.

He ran very fast, and he was soon in front of all the other boys in his class. Then somebody called his name.

He looked round.

Philip was right behind him. Before Joseph knew what was happening, Philip pushed him, very hard, in the back.

Joseph fell over.

He got up at once, but it was too late. Philip ran past him. Philip's friends all clapped loudly and laughed at Joseph.

Later Joseph said to Philip, "You pushed me over."

"Well, I wanted to come first," Philip told him.

"That wasn't fair," said Joseph.

"Nobody saw it happen," said Philip. "Are you going to tell the teacher? You'll be sorry if you do. I shall say that I never pushed you."

Joseph thought that the day would never finish. When at last it was time for the other pupils to go home, Joseph had to stay in the classroom.

Philip came to see him before he left. He was smiling nastily.

"Do you know what I'm going to do now?" he asked.

"No," said Joseph. He wanted Philip to go away.

"You'll never guess, so I'll tell you," Philip went on. "I'm going out in my father's boat."

Philip's father had a boat with an engine. He was not a fisherman, but he sometimes took Philip out fishing, just for fun.

"That's dangerous," Joseph answered. "That boat's too big for you. Does your father know you're going out alone?"

"My father's away," said Philip. "So he won't know about it. And who said I was going alone? I'm going to take a friend out for a ride."

"What friend?" asked Joseph.

"An American friend."

"What American friend?"

"An American boy who lives in a house near ours," said Philip. "His father likes me. I'm going to take my friend to the beach. Then we'll go for a ride in my father's boat."

Chapter 6

It was hot in the classroom, and Joseph was tired and thirsty. It had been a very long day.

But poor Joseph still had a lot of work to do. First, he had to draw a map for his teacher. Then he had to write a story for the headmaster. The story was called, "How to be a good pupil."

At last Joseph finished his story. When the headmaster came into the classroom he gave Joseph a piece of paper.

"You can go home now, Joseph," he said. "But here are some sums. I want you to do all these sums when you get home. Bring them to me tomorrow morning."

Joseph set off for home. The sun was very hot and Joseph walked slowly. His bag felt very heavy.

He felt very sorry for himself. If only he had a bicycle he could be home in no time at all.

Joseph walked through the town. Musa and Salim, two of his friends from school, were waiting for him. They were sitting on a wall, beside the gate to the harbour. Joseph always walked past the harbour gate on his way home.

The two boys were eating mangoes. "Hey, these are good, Joseph," called Musa. "Come and eat. We've saved a mango for you."

"No," said Joseph. "I can't stop. The headmaster gave me some more sums to do at home. If I stop I shall never get home and finish them."

"Listen to this then," said Salim, his other friend. "I've got a new bell for my bicycle. Listen to it for a minute! Do you like it?"

Salim rang the bicycle bell. Joseph felt sad. He wished he had a bicycle like Salim. He listened to the bell, and tried to smile. It was no good.

"I must go home now," he said at last. "I must do these sums. It's all because of Philip. He threw my pencil box through the headmaster's window, but the headmaster thought I did it. It's not fair."

"Philip's a nasty boy," said Musa. "Perhaps something nasty will happen to him, one day."

Joseph walked on. In the harbour, men were loading tins and boxes onto a ship from Zanzibar. Joseph stopped to watch. What would it be like to sail on a ship to Zanzibar, he wondered? Uncle Juma had told him stories about the old trading ships which carried spices and mangrove wood north all the way to the Arab countries.

A sharp cry from a street trader brought Joseph back from his dream. He remembered all his problems. He must hurry home.

"Everything has gone wrong today. If I stop now, I won't finish those sums. Then the headmaster will be angry. Then I shall be in even more trouble. Then everything will go wrong tomorrow too."

But he was also thinking, "It's not fair. Perhaps I won't do the sums. Perhaps I'll do just what I like. Just like Philip!"

He took off his school shoes and walked along the beach. The sea was dark blue. Little waves broke softly against the golden sand. It was beautiful.

There were boys and girls on the beach. Some were playing football or digging in the sand. Others were jumping in the water or swimming.

At the far end of the beach Joseph could see Philip with a little white boy.

"That must be the American boy," Joseph said to himself.

Joseph looked for his uncle by the fishermen's boats. He could not see his uncle's boat anywhere.

"I wish I could go out now and catch a big fish," Joseph thought. "But Uncle Juma has gone without me."

He remembered some of the things he had done with his uncle. Sometimes he had rowed the boat with the oars. Sometimes he had helped pull in the net full of fish.

Once, he had seen his uncle catch a very big fish with his fishing spear. The fish had splashed around in the water, trying to get rid of the sharp spear in its side. His uncle had thrown a net over the fish and pulled it into the boat.

But today there was no fishing. Joseph only had his bag of books, and sums to finish later.

He could see the roof of the mosque far away. He still had a long walk before he got home.

Chapter 7

When Joseph got home his mother was cooking. She often made cakes and sold them in the market. Then the family had a little more money.

"They look good," said Joseph.

He put his bag down on a chair and sat down on the kitchen step. He felt very unhappy.

"Mother," he said. "If you make a lot of cakes, will there be enough money for a bicycle?"

Mrs Kuleba laughed.

"I make cakes so that we have enough money for food and clothes for this family," she told him. "I make cakes so I can buy school uniforms and books and all the other things we need. I don't make cakes so I can buy bicycles."

"But I was late for school again today. I got into trouble. I need a bicycle."

"You need to get up early and hurry," his mother answered.

"Philip has a bicycle," said Joseph quietly.

"Philip has a rich father. He has a car, and a big house, and a boat. Your father's not rich. There will be no bicycle for you, Joseph. You'll just have to walk to school a bit faster."

"Salim at school has a bicycle," Joseph went on. "And his father's not rich."

"Well, he must be richer than we are," she said. "Joseph, that's enough. Stop talking about bicycles."

Joseph suddenly felt very angry. Today had been awful, and now it was nearly over. Why should he stay in? Why should he do all those sums? Why shouldn't he have some fun?

"I'm going to the beach now," he said.

"Well, put your school bag away before you go," said Mrs Kuleba. She lifted it off the chair and passed it to him.

"Why is it so heavy?" she asked.

Joseph did not know what to say.

His mother opened the bag and looked inside.

"Why is there so much paper in here?" she asked.

"The headmaster gave me some sums to do..." Joseph began.

Then Mrs Kuleba pulled something out of the bag. It was the wallet which he had found that morning.

"Joseph!" she said. "Where did you get this? You didn't steal it, did you?"

Joseph had forgotten all about the wallet. It had been in his bag all day, but he had not remembered it.

"No!" he cried. "I don't steal things. I picked it up on my way to school. It was in the grass at the side of the road, near the school."

"Why didn't you give this wallet to the headmaster?" asked his mother. "You should have given it to him as soon as you got to school."

"I wasn't going to keep it," said Joseph. "It's in my bag because I forgot it."

His mother looked inside the wallet. There was a card inside, with a name written on it in black letters. The name was *Robert Steven*.

Robert Steven's address was also written on the card. The street, and the house number were printed below the name. She showed it to Joseph.

"Take this wallet back to this man right now," said his mother. "He must be very worried about it. There's a lot of money here."

"I can take it tomorrow, on my way to school," said Joseph. "I have to go past that street."

"Do it now," said his mother. "But take your school uniform off first. Put on your old shorts and take the wallet back to Robert Steven. Then come back and do your sums."

Joseph went to take off his school uniform. He did not want to walk straight to Robert Steven's house. It was too hot, it was too far, and he was too angry.

He held the wallet in his hand and set off along the beach.

"All my friends can play on the beach but I have to do sums," he said to himself. "Now I have to walk all the way over to this man's house. Then I have to walk all the way back. It's not fair."

Chapter 8

Joseph started to walk towards the sea. He began to dream a little.

"If I had a bicycle I should be at Robert Steven's house in no time."

Some of the boys were still playing football on the beach. One of them threw the ball into the water. Another boy ran into the sea to get it back. Soon the boys were playing a game with the ball in the water.

Further out to sea, near the big waves, Joseph saw a boat. There were two boys in it. One was a little white boy.

"That must be Philip and his American friend," Joseph said to himself.

Joseph had been out to sea with his Uncle Juma, and knew the waves were dangerous. He remembered the sharks too, with their big teeth. They were even more dangerous than the waves.

"Philip's foolish to go out so far," he thought.

"Come on," shouted the boys with the ball. "Come and play."

Joseph badly wanted to join in. Should he swim with the other boys? It would not take very long. He could just stay in the sea for a few minutes. And perhaps Ben would help him with his sums.

Just then somebody called out to him.

"Hello, Joseph."

It was Uncle Juma. He was carrying three big silvery fish in an old basket.

"I waited for you when the other children came out of school," said Uncle Juma. "What happened?"

"I'm sorry. I had to stay at school."

"Do you want to come out in the boat later on? I can't take you now because I have to go into town. I'm going to sell these fish to one of the cooks in the market. I won't be long though."

"Why can't I have some fun?" Joseph thought to himself. "I've had an awful day, with nothing but trouble."

"Yes please," the words came out.

That was it! He was going to swim and then he was going to go fishing. He was going to forget all about sums and wallets and he was going to have some fun.

"Will you look after this wallet for me?" Joseph asked quickly. "It will be safe with you, Uncle Juma. It belongs to a man who lives near the school. I'll take it back to him later on."

Uncle Juma took the wallet from Joseph and pushed it into his shirt pocket.

"All right, Joseph. I'll be back soon. Wait for me here after your swim," he said, and he turned and walked away from the beach.

Joseph swam out into the water. It was cool on his hot skin, and he felt better already.

As he swam towards the boys he looked out to sea. He could still see Philip and the little white boy. The little boy was leaning over the side of the boat, looking in the water.

"I hope there are no sharks out there," one of the boys said.

Joseph put his head under the water. He could see pretty little fish swimming around. He loved their bright colours. He tried to catch them with his hands, but they were too quick for him.

Then Joseph began to make his way back to the beach.

"Help! Help!"

What was that? Joseph's ears were full of water and he could not hear very well.

"Help! Help!"

Somebody was shouting for help.

Joseph looked out to sea. There was Philip! He was standing up in his father's boat!

Philip was shouting and the little white boy was crying. People were hurrying to the beach.

"What's happening?"

"What's going on?"

"Look at that boat! The engine's stopped!" cried one of the children on the beach.

"Look at the waves," shouted an old man. "It's dangerous out there."

"What about the sharks? Are there any sharks out there today?"

Joseph thought about the little boy in the boat. He must do something! He ran along the beach until he found his uncle's boat. Luckily it was very close to the water. He pushed the boat as hard as he could. It slipped across the sand and into the sea.

Chapter 9

Joseph climbed into Uncle Juma's boat and sat down among the nets and spears and ropes. He did not have time to throw them over the side.

He picked up a paddle and began to paddle as fast as he could. It was hard work, and soon his arms began to hurt.

He looked quickly out to sea. He was not much nearer to Philip and the little white boy, so he pushed up the little sail, as he had seen his uncle do so many times.

The wind was blowing and the boat moved forward more quickly. He had to save Philip and the little white boy.

As he rowed out to sea the water became rough and the waves were bigger. He was afraid.

"Help! Help!"

He could hear the shouts. He had to go on. "I'm coming, I'm coming."

At last he was near to Philip's boat. The waves were breaking right over it, and Philip and the little boy were both crying.

"Philip!" he called. "Don't worry. I've come to help you."

"How can you help? You're no good! You can't start the engine!"

The waves were getting bigger and bigger all the time.

"Get into my boat," Joseph shouted. "We can row back to the beach."

"I can't, I can't!" called Philip. "I'm afraid."

Then Joseph saw something in the water. What was it? It moved towards the boat. It looked like a big fish – a shark!

Philip and the boy saw it too.

"It's going to crash into the boat! We shall fall out!" cried Philip. "It's going to attack us!"

Joseph had to think fast. He picked up a paddle and tried to hit the shark. He missed the first time, so he tried again.

As he did so a big wave hit the boat.

Joseph dropped the paddle into the sea. He fell over and cut his leg on one of Uncle Juma's spears.

He did not have time to cry. When he stood up the shark was right next to his boat.

He picked up a spear and tried again to hit the shark. This time he hit it very hard, right on the nose. "Bang!"

The spear almost broke, but the shark stayed where it was.

"Crash!"

Joseph hit the shark's nose with the spear again, but still it would not go away.

When another wave came along Joseph could have cried. The shark rolled right over, out of the water. It was not a shark at all! It was not even a fish! It was just some wood, from one of the big ships.

Suddenly Joseph heard an engine.

He turned round, and saw Philip's boat move away. The engine was working again.

"Wait for me!" Joseph called. "You can pull me back to the beach."

Philip waved.

"Sorry, we can't help you," he laughed.

Joseph was very angry.

"You've got to help me!" he called. "I rowed out to help you. I came to save you. You can't just leave me. My arms are tired."

But the engine was too loud and Philip did not hear him.

The people on the beach watched the boats. They could see everything. They watched as Joseph hit something with the paddle.

Then everybody shouted at the same time.

"There's a shark out there! The poor little boy! The shark will attack him!"

They watched Philip's boat pass Joseph and fly through the water to the beach.

"What a nasty boy!" they all shouted. "He left the other boy in the little boat out there, all alone."

"And the sea is very rough."

"And there are sharks out there, and the sharks are dangerous."

Nobody greeted Philip when he got out of his boat. Nobody ran to meet him. Nobody helped him.

Philip did not talk to anybody. He tied up the boat and ran off along the beach.

One old man shouted at Philip, "I'm going to tell your father about you! You are a very naughty boy!"

Chapter 10

While Philip was hurrying along the beach, Joseph was in big trouble. He could not get the boat to sail back towards the land. The wind and the waves were too strong. He was afraid, his leg hurt, and he was very tired.

He almost gave up.

Then he heard a shout. "Joseph!"

It was his Uncle Juma and another fisherman! They had a boat with an engine. They had come to save him.

"Catch this rope!" they called. "Now tie it to the front of your boat."

Joseph tied the rope to the little boat, and Uncle Juma and his friend pulled him slowly to the beach.

Joseph climbed out of the boat and sat down on the sand.

"Thank you, Uncle Juma!" he said. He was too tired to say more.

Uncle Juma did not smile.

"I'm very angry with you, Joseph," he said. "Why did you go out in my boat? It's dangerous for a young boy to play in boats like that."

"I wasn't playing," said Joseph. "I was trying to save Philip."

"What are you talking about? What's this about Philip?" asked his uncle.

"He was out there, in the rough water, in his father's boat. The waves were breaking right over the boat," Joseph said. "I tried to save him."

"Was he the boy in the boat with the engine?" asked Uncle Juma. "Why did you need to save him?"

Joseph told him the whole story.

"I was afraid the shark would attack," he finished. "But it wasn't a shark at all. It was just some wood from one of the big ships."

"That was very lucky," said Uncle Juma. "I know you only wanted to help, but you did everything wrong. You must never go out alone like that."

"I was trying to help." Joseph wanted to cry. "And now I'm tired and my leg hurts. And I've just remembered. I've still got to take that wallet back."

He held out his hand.

"Can I have the wallet, please?"

His uncle put his hand in his pocket.

He took it out again. It was empty.

"It's gone!" he said. "I'm sorry, Joseph. I must have dropped it."

Uncle Juma scratched his head.

"Oh no!" Joseph said. "Now I shall be in even more trouble. Everything's gone wrong today. Everybody's angry with me. I haven't done my sums, I'm tired and my leg hurts. And now the wallet's lost."

Uncle Juma sat down next to Joseph.

"Let me think," he said. "I'm sure it was still in my pocket when I left the market. Yes, it was. I did hurry along the beach, when I saw my boat was gone. Yes, that's it. I must have dropped it on the beach."

"I must go and look for it!" Joseph said quickly. "I told my mother I would take it back."

"Wait a minute and I'll help you," said Uncle Juma. "I'll just pull the boat out of the water."

"No!" cried Joseph.

He ran off along the beach. "I can't wait. I must find the wallet now!"

Joseph could not hurry for long. He was very tired and his arms and legs hurt.

Soon he was walking slowly along the road by the beach, under the trees. As he walked along he looked down. The wallet must be somewhere. He had to find it. It must be there somewhere, near the path by the beach

He could not see the wallet anywhere.

"I should have waited for Uncle Juma," he thought. "He must know where to look. After all, he lost the wallet."

He walked up from the beach, a little way towards the market, and then came back. All the time he looked at the ground. There was nothing there, except dust and grass and stones.

He was still looking down when he saw two feet in front of him. That was all he could see at first. When he looked up, he saw who the feet belonged to.

They belonged to Philip.

Chapter 11

"Hello, Joseph," said Philip. "What are you doing here?"

"I'm looking for something," said Joseph.

"What are you looking for?" asked Philip.

"I'm not telling you," said Joseph.

He did not want to tell Philip about the wallet. Philip might find it and keep it.

"Were you looking for this?" Philip said.

He held out the wallet.

"How did you know?" asked Joseph. "Where did you get it?"

"I saw your uncle drop it," said Philip with a nasty smile. "He ran past me on the beach. He was running to save you and he dropped it. I saw it all."

"Good," said Joseph. "Now please give me the wallet. I found it. My uncle was only looking after it for me. I'm going to give it back."

"No," said Philip.

"Why not?" asked Joseph. "It isn't yours. You can't keep it."

"I'm not going to keep it," said Philip. "I'm going to take it to Mr Robert Steven. It's his wallet. I know him anyway."

"What do you mean – you know him?"asked Joseph.

Philip smiled and gave Joseph a knowing look. "He's the father of my American friend."

"Then I'll come with you," said Joseph angrily.

The boys walked across the town to Robert Steven's house. They did not talk. Joseph was tired and Philip walked too fast.

Joseph looked at the houses in the street where Robert Steven lived.

The houses were all very big, with strong gates and beautiful walled gardens around them. Only rich people had enough money to live in this part of town. Joseph was a little bit afraid of the people in the big houses.

A big silver car turned and drove silently through some gates further down the road. It was so quiet here, not like the street where he lived.

The two boys came to a white house with green curtains. There was a gate with the name 'Steven' on it, and behind the gate there was a dog.

Joseph saw the big silver car again. It parked beside the house.

"Does Mr Steven know what happened?" he asked. "Does he know about the engine and the rough sea?"

"No," said Philip. "And if you tell him, I'll beat you. Then you'll be sorry."

Joseph stood by the gate and watched Philip. He did not want to meet the dog. He did not even want to meet Robert Steven now.

"He might think I took the wallet," he said to himself.

A tall white man was getting out of the car. Philip ran up to him.

"Mr Steven," he said. "I've found your wallet! Look!"

The man turned round. Joseph had seen him before, down at the port. "Perhaps he works there," he thought.

Joseph saw the man take the wallet from Philip. He could hear every word that was said.

"Thank you, Philip," said the man.

He smiled at Philip. "You've been very good today. First you looked after my son on the beach. Now you've found my wallet. Where was it?"

"It was in the road, by your gate," Philip said.

This was not true, but Robert Steven did not know that.

"That's funny," said Mr Steven. "I thought I must have lost it on the way to work in the port."

"No, it was near your gate," Philip told him. "But you were lucky. Nobody stole it. Look! There's a young boy there, by the gate. A boy like that might easily steal a wallet."

Joseph did not want to wait by the gate any longer. Philip would not tell Robert Steven what had happened. He would just make up a story.

He started to walk home, very fast. He felt very unhappy.

A minute later he heard somebody behind him. He turned around, to see who was there.

It was Philip, and he was smiling.

"Look at this!" Philip laughed. "Mr Steven gave me a reward because I found his wallet."

He waved a clean, new bank-note under Joseph's nose.

"You should give me some of that," Joseph told him. "I found that wallet first."

"But you lost it. And you didn't come with me to give the money back," said Philip.

He laughed again. "So the money's mine."

He ran off down the road.

Joseph shouted after him, "One day, somebody will find out all about you, Philip! Then you'll be sorry!"

Joseph walked back along the beach, past the fishing boats. It was already nearly dark. He hurried as fast as he could. He was hungry and he still had to do the sums the headmaster had given him.

Today had been a really bad day.

Chapter 12

When Joseph got home, his mother was just putting the food on the table. His little sister was fetching salt from the cupboard. The whole family was there, except for Ben.

"Come and eat, Joseph," said Mrs Kuleba.

"May I water my tomatoes first?" asked Joseph. He did not want to talk to anybody for a while.

"Yes, but be quick," his mother answered.

Joseph filled a bucket with water. He carried it out onto the balcony.

His leg was still hurting him, and he wanted to be alone, just for a minute.

Joseph sat down. It was quiet on the roof. He thought about everything that had happened that day.

"It started as a bad day," he thought. "And it went on that way. It's not fair. Boys like Philip never have bad days."

He picked a little black fly off one of the tomato plants. He was still thinking hard.

"Even so, Philip doesn't have many friends," he thought. "Most people who are friends with Philip are afraid of him. They're not real friends. Not like Salim and Musa."

He felt a bit better now. He got up to water his plants. He lifted the bucket, but he couldn't see very well in the dark and he knocked one of the pots over.

The pot fell off the balcony and down into the street below with a big crash.

Then somebody shouted, "Ei! Who did that?"

Joseph looked down into the street. Ben was standing there with his bicycle. In the light from the doorway, Joseph could see leaves and tomatoes and broken bits of pot all around.

Ben looked very funny.

Joseph wanted to laugh, but he did not. After all, Ben might be angry with him. He went inside, and soon he heard Ben's feet on the stairs.

When Ben sat down at the table he said nothing. Joseph could not be quiet any longer.

"Please don't be angry about the tomato plant, Ben," he begged. "It was an accident. And I've had a very bad day."

"I'm not angry," Ben answered. "Why was your day so bad?"

Joseph told the whole family about everything that had gone wrong.

When he finished his story everybody began to speak at once.

"You should get up early and hurry to school," said his mother. "If you had been with all the other children, the dog would have run away. It wouldn't have chased you up the tree."

"And Philip wouldn't have taken your pencil box," added his father.

"And your teacher wouldn't have been angry," said his little sister.

"And the headmaster wouldn't have kept you in school," said his father.

"You should have remembered the wallet," his mother told him.

"You should have given it to the headmaster at once," said his little sister.

"It was dangerous to go out in the boat," said his mother.

"And you should never ask your Uncle Juma to look after anything," said his father. "He never keeps anything safe."

"Stop," said Joseph. "Please stop!"

Everybody looked at Joseph, and then they began to laugh.

"Poor Joseph," said Ben at last. "He's had a very bad day. But now I have some news. For me, it's been a good day."

They all looked at Ben.

"What's your good news?" asked his mother.

"I have a job," Ben told them. There was a big smile on his face. "I'm going to work on one of the big ships. I shall have to leave home but I shall come back often."

Everyone was quiet. Was it true? A job? If Ben had a job that was good. If the big ship took him far away, that was bad.

Nobody knew whether to be happy or sad.

At last Mr Kuleba said, "Well done, Ben."

"That's very good news, Ben," his mother said. Then she added, "But I'm sorry that you have to go away."

"I'm even more sorry," said Joseph. "I need you to help me with my school work!"

Then everybody laughed again.

"Well," said Ben. "I want to ask you something, Joseph."

"What's that?"

Ben smiled. "Will you do something for me?"

"Well . . ."

"Will you?" Ben asked again. "Say yes or no."

"Oh very well," said Joseph. "As long as it's not too difficult, I'll do it. What do you want?"

"I want you to look after my bicycle."

"What? Your bicycle? Me? Why?"

All the family laughed at Joseph. He looked down at the floor. He really was very sad because Ben was going away. But to have a bicycle! Could it be true?

"Don't be sad, Joseph," said Ben. "I'll write to you from all the exciting places the big ship goes to. And you can think of me when you ride my bicycle."

"Yes," said Joseph slowly.

As the family went on eating, he began to dream. He dreamed of riding Ben's bicycle in the cool evening, down by the port. He would look at the big ships. Ben would be on one of those big ships. Ben would go all over the world, and when he came back there would be so many stories to tell . . .

Ben's voice broke into his dream. "Finish your supper, Joseph. Then I'll help you with your sums."

Today was nearly over. Joseph breathed deeply.

"Tomorrow will be better," he thought, and he smiled.

The very next day, Joseph rode Ben's bicycle to school for the first time. He had finished all his sums, and they were with his pencil box and his library book, in his bag.

It was still quite early when he arrived at the school gate. Only a few boys were in the school yard.

As he got off his bicycle, he saw a big silver car stop outside the school gate. A man and a boy were inside it.

Joseph looked at the car and the people inside.

The man was Robert Steven. The little boy was the one who had been with Philip yesterday.

The little boy waved and smiled at Joseph. Robert Steven leaned out of the window, and called Joseph over.

"Harry – that's my son here – told me what happened at the beach yesterday," Mr Steven said. "You are a very brave boy. Harry would like to say a big thank you. Can you come to our house this afternoon, after school?"

"It's my birthday, today," explained the little boy. "Do you like birthday cake?"

"Yes I do," said Joseph happily.

He looked down at Ben's bicycle, and he thought for a moment.

"Can you ride a bicycle, Harry?" he asked.

"No – well, not yet," said Harry, with a shy smile.

"Then I will teach you, just like my brother Ben taught me!" laughed Joseph.

And he did.

Already available in **Mactracks**

Starters

The Hunter's Dream Meja Mwangi
Martha's Mistakes Lorna Evans
Martha's Big News Lorna Evans
Fiki Learns to Like Other People Lauretta Ngcobo
Zulu Spear Olive Langa
Mercy in a Hurry Mary Harrison
Tanzai and Bube John Haynes
Karabo's Accident Frances Cross
The Little Apprentice Tailor Marcus Kamara
Follow that Footprint! Jill Inyundo
We're Still Moving! Damian Morgan
Tomorrow Will Be Better Akberali Manji
Voices in the Night Erna Müller
How Does Your Body Work? Lorna Evans *(information book)*

Sprinters

Mystery of the Sagrenti Treasure Ekow Yarney
Eyes and Ears Brenda Ferry
Eyes and Ears Work Hard Brenda Ferry
One in a Million Emma Johnson
Map on the Wall Colin Swatridge
Magic Trees Jenny Vincent
Dark Blue is for Dreams Rosina Umelo
Danger in the Palace Grace Nkansa
Granny Sangoma John Byrne
Axarob's Secret Dawn Ridgway
The Past Tells a Story Lorna Evans (*information book*)
You Can Draw! John Byrne (*information book*)

Runners

Guitar Wizard Walije Gondwe
Star Nandi Dlovu
Days of Silence Rosina Umelo
Never Leave Me Hope Dube
Juwon's Battle Victor Thorpe
Fineboy Maurice Sotabinda
Front Page Story John Byrne
Crocodile Challenge James Ngumy

Winners

Halima Meshack Asare
Foli Fights the Forgers Kofi Quaye
Jojo in New York Kofi Quaye
Presents from Mr Bakare Mary Harrison
Sara's Friends Rosina Umelo
Trouble in the City Hope Dube
Sunbird's Paradise James Ngumy
Kayo's House Barbara Kimenye
Secret Fear Mohamed Sheriff
Be Beautiful Lydia Eagle and Barbara Jackson (*information book*)
Sport in Africa Ossie Stuart (*information book*)